'Roedd yn y wlad honno
The shepherds were keeping their watch

Welsh traditional words
English translation: Jonathan Jones

Original melody: Dr Caradog Roberts
arr. Louis Halsey

4

Choral Programme Series
Consultant Editor: Simon Halsey

Five Welsh Carols
Pump Carol Cymraeg

'ROEDD YN Y WLAD HONNO
The shepherds were keeping their watch

TUA BETHL'EM DREF
Come from ev'ry land

O DEUED POB CRISTION
Come all Christians, singing

SEREN BETHLEHEM
Dark the night

OER YW'R GŴR SY'N METHU CARU
Deck the hall with boughs of holly

(SATB/organ or piano)

ARRANGED BY LOUIS HALSEY

FABER *ff* MUSIC

CONTENTS

PRONUNCIATION

To aid your pronunciation of the Welsh in this volume,
we recommend the following publication (available with or without cassette):
Colloquial Welsh by Gary King, published by Routledge (1995).

© 1999 by Faber Music Ltd
First published in 1999 by Faber Music Ltd
3 Queen Square London WC1N 3AU
Music processed by Silverfen
Printed in England by Halstan & Co Ltd
All rights reserved

ISBN 0-571-51925-3

To buy Faber Music publications or to find out about the full range of titles available
please contact your local retailer or Faber Music sales enquiries:

Tel: +44 (0)1279 82 89 82
Fax: +44 (0)1279 82 89 83
E-mail: sales@fabermusic.co.uk
Website: www.fabermusic.co.uk

Yn lân__ wed-i'u__ ca - nu yng ngwerth-fawr__ waed__
From sin__ He has__ freed you, and there__ He will

baedd - u'n__ y byd;_____
gar - ments__ of white:_____

Ie - su, Er maint__ fu__ i'w__ baedd - u'n y__ byd,_____ y
greet you And clothe__ you__ in__ gar - ments of__ white,___ of

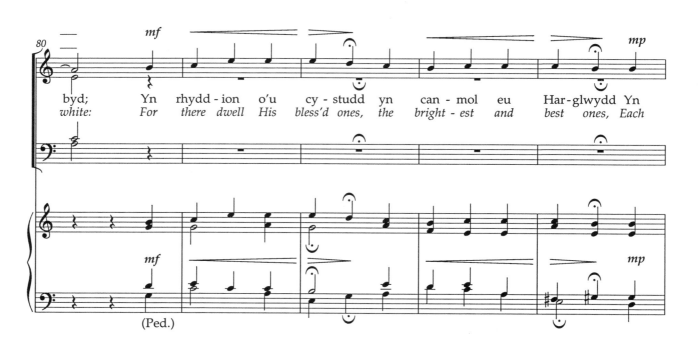

byd; Yn rhydd - ion o'u cy - studd yn can - mol eu Har-glwydd Yn
white: For there dwell His bless'd ones, the bright - est and best ones, Each

(Ped.)

car - io hardd balm-wydd bob un _____ Mewn teyr - nas _ uwch _
bear - ing a palm in his hand; _____ *Re - leased _ from _ all _*

dae - ar, fel haul _ yn _ dra hawdd - gar, Heb gar - char na _
suff - 'ring, His glad _ prais - es _ off - 'ring, They _ dwell _ in _ the _

ga - lar _ na _ gwŷn, na gwŷn; A'r bach - gen _ bach _
hea - ven - ly _ land, hea - ven - ly _ land. And Him _ who _ they _

(Ped.)

Tua Bethl'em dref

Come from ev'ry land

Welsh words: Wil Ifan
English translation: Jonathan Jones

Original melody: Edward Arthur
arr. Louis Halsey

Ped.

Y___ Tra - gwy - ddol Air,
The___ E - ter - nal One,

Y Tra - gwy - ddol Air,
The E - ter - nal One,

2. I Fach - ge - nnyn Mair,
2. Ma - ry's lit - tle son,

2. I Fach - ge - nnyn Mair,
2. Ma - ry's lit - tle son,

Yn _ y _ gwellt_a'r _ gwair,
Ly - ing_ in ___ the _ hay;

Dy - gwn ___ rodd-ion: Serch y ___ ga - lon,
Praise we ___ sing Him, Gifts we ___ bring Him,

14

3. Aur an - rhe - gion_ Thus a myrr,   Tu - a Beth - lem dref_
3. Gold we_ of - fer,_ In - cense, myrrh.   Come from ev - 'ry land,_

Aur_____ an-
Gold_____ we

Man.

Awn_ yn_ fin - tai gref,_ Ac a - ddo - lwn
Join_ the_ migh - ty band,_ Come_ to_ Beth - le -

Ped.

Ef,   Ac a - ddo - lwn_ Ef.
-hem,   Come_ to_ Beth - le_ hem.

(senza rall.)

Man.

O deued pob Cristion

Come all Christians, singing

Welsh traditional words
English translation: verse 1 A. G. Prys-Jones
            verse 2 Jonathan Jones

Welsh traditional melody
arr. Louis Halsey

Seren Bethlehem

Dark the night

Welsh traditional words
English translation: K. E. Roberts

Original melody: Canon Owen Jones
arr. Louis Halsey

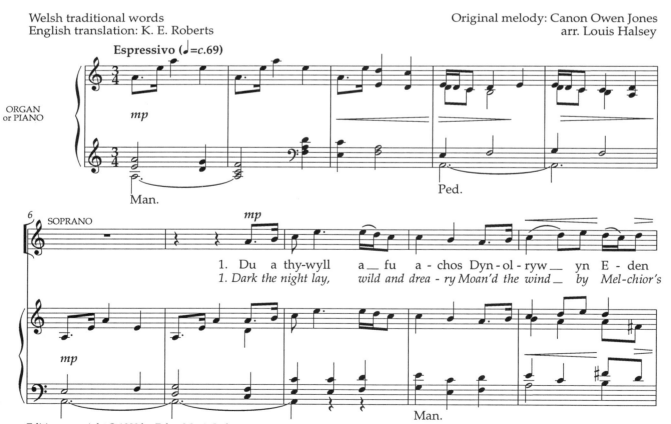

1. Du a thy-wyll a fu a-chos Dyn-ol-ryw yn E - den
1. *Dark the night lay, wild and drea - ry Moan'd the wind by Mel-chior's*

Oer yw'r gŵr sy'n methu caru (Nos Galan)

Deck the hall with boughs of holly

Welsh traditional words
Author of English words unknown

Welsh traditional melody
arr. Louis Halsey

Pump Carol Cymraeg

Y mae pump o'r carolau Cymraeg mwyaf atgofus a thelynegol wedi cael eu trefnu yma ġan Louis Halsey. Y mae'r trefniadau crefftus hyn, ynglyn â throsiadau canu Saesneġ, yn addas i'r rhan fwyaf o ġorau, ac y maent yn rhoi cyfle iddyn nhw i archwilio trysorau un o'r cenhedloedd mwyaf cerddorol y byd.

Trwy hud y cywair lleiaf yn 'Roedd yn y wlad honno a Seren Bethlehem, tuag at uchafbwynt y casgliad, Oer yw'r ġŵr sy'n methu caru ġellir perfformio'r carolau hyn naill ai ar wahân neu ġyda'u ġilydd.

Five Welsh Carols

Five of the most lyrical and atmospheric Welsh carols are here beautifully arranged by Louis Halsey. Expertly crafted and well within the grasp of most choirs, these arrangements, complete with fresh English singing translations, offer choirs the chance to explore treasures from one of the most musical of nations.

Through the minor-key magic of 'Roedd yn y wlad honno and Seren Bethlehem to the climax of the collection, Oer yw'r ġŵr sy'n methu caru ('Deck the hall with boughs of holly'), these carols can either be performed separately or as a group.

❅ ❅ ❅

The Faber Music Choral Programme Series

The acclaimed Choral Programme Series provides a wealth of invaluable concert repertoire for upper voice choirs, including works by Brahms, Holst, Bridge, Stanford, Warlock, Fauré, Saint-Saëns, Schubert and Schumann, as well as Christmas repertoire, gospel choruses, arrangements of folk songs and hits from the shows.

Other Christmas volumes for mixed voices

Benjamin Britten *Christ's Nativity*	ISBN 0-571-51513-4
Baroque Christmas Classics: Bach, Praetorius, Schütz etc.	ISBN 0-571-51697-1
A Christmas Celebration – Eleven carols from Georgian England	ISBN 0-571-51792-7
Classic French Carols (arr. Trepte)	ISBN 0-571-51684-X
A Gospel Christmas – Spirituals for the festive season (arr. Runswick)	ISBN 0-571-51514-2
My Dancing Day – Five English carols (arr. Trepte)	ISBN 0-571-51858-3
Three German Carols (arr. Trepte)	ISBN 0-571-51857-5
Merry Christmas Everybody! – Five Christmas pop classics	ISBN 0-571-51859-1

ISBN 0-571-519

FABER MUSIC · 3 QUEEN SQUARE · LONDON

9 780571 519255